This journal belongs to

Welcome

When we look at Earth, and all of existence, it is easy to see an abundant flow of creativity, unerring beauty and endless possibility. The essence that powers stars and opens flowers is present in everything – including you. By connecting with the earth, we remember our own divinity and enliven the creativity, beauty and possibilities that are innate within us all.

To understand our own nature, we can turn to the very earth we have risen from. The more we know about the world around us, the greater understanding we have of ourselves and the myriad strategies, perspectives and responses available to us at any given moment.

Humanity has long turned to nature for answers. By watching the skies, the seasons, the plants and the animals around us, we can make predictions about our environment that will reduce hardship and improve our chances of survival. We continue to turn to nature for solutions in design, medicine, organisation, systems and much more. Whatever the problem, somewhere in its vast history, our Sacred Earth has already solved it.

The seeker is the finder

When we look for answers, we will find them … in the same way as searching for gold may lead to the discovery of quartz or granite (and vice versa). When looking for a lost item, we can find all manner of misplaced, forgotten or unexpected treasures. We don't always find what we started looking for, but instead come across other valuables. If Alexander Fleming hadn't been looking for something, we might not have penicillin.

If a lost item is something essential, like car keys, we persist with the search until we find it. At the end of the hunt, we may have upturned coins, jewellery, photographs, memorabilia, phone numbers and odd socks! On the way to finding a new job, your search may reveal a latent talent, trigger a forgotten connection or bring your self-doubt to the surface so you can acknowledge and heal it.

The search for love, understanding, peace, freedom or inspiration is never fruitless. As a seeker, you will make many powerful discoveries. If you don't stumble across treasure easily, quickly or in the way you had planned, don't let that stop you. Under the next rock, in the next tunnel, across the next horizon – or the one after that – your gold is surely waiting. Keep upturning, digging and expanding until you get there. Be wise and keep seeking!

Step outside

Honour the seeker in you by stepping outside of expectation and letting go of constraint. Let the clouds open so inky rain pours over these pages. Let your expression flow in streams of consciousness. Let it come slowly. Let it deepen. Let it puddle, let it rage, let it trickle. Each mark on the page falls and waters a seed so that your sketches, lyrics, memories, plans, poems, notes, heartaches, hopes and musings grow to become a rich and vibrant landscape – a landscape where the dandelions aren't competing, the mountains aren't jealous of the sea and the rain doesn't come on schedule. Yours is the rain, the sun and the seeds. You are the creator, but also the observer. Open your journal, and step outside of judgement, comparison and timetables. Go outside of who you understand yourself to be.

Whatever happens in this space is not housed by concepts of good or bad. It just is. And, because of that freedom, journaling may not garner results that are obvious, expected or hoped for. Instead, it will expand your perspective, deepen your insight, inspire creativity and champion your relationship with yourself and your world. It might also take you to places you would rather avoid.

In the way that a casual walk in the bush might turn into a battle with the undergrowth if we followed our whims rather than the beaten track, journaling can be uncomfortable. Unpleasant or unfamiliar feelings, thoughts and realisations are part of the process. They are the reason journaling is so valuable. If anger, shame, jealousy, doubt or pain arises, do not retreat behind the walls of shoulds and should nots. Stand in the rain, continue to explore and, remember, you are safe here.

Getting started

Expressing yourself can bring you to a richer understanding of yourself. We don't always know how we feel, what we would like or who we should be in a situation. Coming to our feelings, likes and identity can take time. And your feelings, likes and other aspects of who you are can and will change. Therefore, journaling is not something to perfect, but something to practice. In time, your scribblings will fall into their own current. The hardest part can be making it over the first hump and getting started. This journal has written and visual components that may help with that. They can be used as prompts or trigger points for reflection or creativity. Here are a few suggestions on how to start your pen moving:

- Turn to any page and choose a single word that stands out for you. Write it somewhere on a page, and then surround it with memories, words or feelings you associate with it.

- Select a phrase at random. Argue for it and against it. Can you think of an example from your own experience when it was true? Can you think of a time when it was false? Is there a truth that encompasses both positions?

- Open the journal to one of the images. Helena Nelson-Reed's artwork is full of symbology. Find a symbol you aren't familiar with or don't know the meaning of. Copy that or another symbol and colour it in whatever hues you choose. Repeat the drawing in different colours or sizes and see where it takes you.

- Write a short story, poem or memory to match one of the images.

- Make lists. Holiday destinations, embarrassing moments, top qualities, people you hope to grow closer to, things you would like to try … anything at all.

- Have a dialogue with your pens. For example, if you are in two minds about something, make a black pen take one side and a blue pen the other. You might ascribe aspects of yourself to different pens and have a conversation with your inner child, rebel or sage.

- Record your dreams, your card readings or your meditations.

- Engage your senses. I bet you can quickly recall the smell of a rainforest or the taste of the ocean. We are always hearing, seeing, touching, smelling and tasting the world around us, but are not always conscious of it. What does driving your car taste like? What does checking your emails smell like? Does folding the laundry have a melody? What colour was a discussion? What flavour is a memory?

- Look for new ways to tell past stories.

Our Sacred Earth is a healer, a teacher and a muse. Consciously connecting to this tremendous resource can awaken us to deeper truths and bring us closer to divinity. Just being in nature is enough to deepen our humility, gratitude and awe. Communing with our living planet can be transformative.

Through the wisdom, love and sanctity of Earth, the dull, monotony of the mundane can transform into a rich chorus of splendour. From the colour and form of the artwork, to the beat and sound of the text, this journal is here to expand your experience of our planet and yourself as divinely wise and loving beings. It comes with the reminder that we are all connected. What Earth knows, you can know. What you know, the world can know.

Enjoy!

Leela

Within the garden of your heart a beautiful soul exists
that beautiful soul is you

This moment
with no beginning or end
no point of entry

no leaving
coming or going
just uncontainable life

unpredictable
like these words
trying to express the inexpressible

like light flickering through clouds of illusion
like a flame glowing inside us
and every leaf and blade of grass

for we are all flames of the sacred fire
burning our way through time
and all that lies beyond it

we are this most sacred Earth
and air
and water

the faint memory
of an ancient sun
that still glows inside us

and crimson leaves
falling through
gold light

— Toni Carmine Salerno

"If we wish to understand the nature of the universe, we have an inner hidden advantage: we are ourselves little portions of the universe and so carry the answer within us."

— Jacques Boivin

In the absence of light, we find safety, formation, growth, healing and intimacy. Don't fight the darkness. Welcome it and let it embrace you. When you are ready, rested and healed, you can emerge from your chrysalis and spread your wings once more.

Absence makes the soul grow stronger. The absence of agenda, stress
or the need to wear a mask opens the way for presence.

It is up to you to acknowledge an obstacle as impermanent.
Regardless of who is to blame, it is your responsibility to defy a false limitation.

A quirk or idiosyncrasy is a strength. Bring it out and own it. Individuality is a precious gem. Throw your woes into the smelting pot and craft them into powerful tools. Experiment with what you have and give it value.

Even the most steadfast, most long-standing objects formed in our planet's infancy can be transformed. Do not accept anything as a given.

Use the alchemical fire at your core to transform any tenacious, hindering habits, doubts or beliefs into precious gems. Turn lead into gold. Let your greater self surface — refine, polish and respect its beauty, strength and value.

Diamond is the hardest natural mineral on our planet. Graphite is one of the softest. Both are pure carbon. In graphite, the atoms bond in two-dimensional layers. In diamonds, the atoms bond in a three-dimensional lattice to make connections on all sides, not just to its 'neighbours' on the same plane. Our ability to make diverse and involved connections makes us strong.

You are in every word, every leaf and part of every star.
You are the love that underpins the all. Bring this connection to consciousness.

The impact of even a small change can ripple across every area of your life.

Go forth and make mistakes. Learn from them and prosper.

Open yourself to the light of the world. Draw it into you,
be empowered by it and channel it into your environment for
all to benefit from. Face all that comes your way and trust your
ability to make change for the greater good.

My Blue Shadow

The soul casts its infinite blue shadow over the earth
Time awakens something in the heart
Like a dream that fits not into words
Something is missing
Someone is searching
For something that never was missing
Life, the earth and stars …
Everything we see is a reflection of a reflection
A projection of the divine nature within us
I cast my shadow over the earth
Not knowing it was blue
What a wonderful colour ...
I am so close to you now
For these words transcend time and space
I am so close and yet so far – even from myself
For heaven and earth rarely meet
Too many reflections get in the way
Too many projections ...
We are all far from everything
We are all part of everything
We are one, yet divided into infinite parts
How strange life is
How amazing and confusing
Who would have thought that a shadow could be blue ...?

– Toni Carmine Salerno

Step outside conformity and well-meaning advice and generate a creative solution through conversation, determination, experimentation and play.

*Much is accomplished with seemingly little effort when love and
purpose are on your side.*

Not everything we think up is destined for this time and place.
Just like lightning, most ideas will never ground, but when they
strike the right mix of elements, they can be world changing.

Most lightning occurs within the clouds, but when it does ground,
it can strike the same place, not just twice but many times over.
When one idea strikes, many more are likely to follow.

Generate brilliance!

Do not confuse selfishness with self-centring. Bring your wellbeing, your values, your future and your loves to the centre of your world. Being centred makes you stronger and more balanced, and disturbances are less likely to knock you off course. Centre and extend your positive sphere of influence.

An invisible force gently pushes and pulls you towards your true centre.
Let go and let it flow. It has been a long journey, but the destination
is so much closer than you think.

We come into this world with love at our centre, but disturbances can knock us from our orbit. When this happens, our centre of gravity can shift, and we might settle into lesser orbits, circling around all manner of people, values and expectations. But love is the brightly-burning sun at the true centre of your world, and its invisible pull brings you ever closer to her glorious light.

Follow love to the peaceful space inside your heart.
It is your power centre, from which all is possible, and all is available.

A leaf is falling
smiling at the clouds
in total freedom
and trust
the divine nature
holds all in its embrace
in the heart of a bustling city
in the soul of a forest
a glowing ray shines through
a lonely seagull glides over the ocean
while the desert sings its soulful song
a whisper
a cry
a child is born
and someone sheds a tear of joy
while
somewhere else
someone else
cries tears of sadness
the world goes on turning
the divine nature is present in all things.

— Toni Carmine Salerno

Most diamonds were formed far beneath the earth's surface. It takes a deep eruption to bring these gems to the surface, where they can be discovered and marvelled at. Your base values are stored deep within you, crystallising in isolation, far away from external elements. During turmoil or trauma, these precious gems can surface, bringing you surprising, invaluable clarity.

Find yourself by losing yourself in a conversation, a story, a melody or someone's eyes.

Be vulnerable, be emotional and be moved to deeper understanding. Let the pain, suffering, love and joy of others find a home in your heart. Accepting another without reservation is accepting yourself.

Separation from the energy, beauty, grace and power of the Divine Mother is an illusion. Feel her fertility and everlasting peace inside you. Through her love, life unfolds with endless blessings. Her love flows within and through you, out into the world.

A drop of water falls, repeats its story of tears, icicles, water pistols, rapids, storms, sweat and rapture, until it is welcomed into its ocean home once more. The drop is no longer. Its boundaries are no more. And yet, nothing is lost. You too are on a journey home. Every cell of your being knows the way, and your destination is guaranteed.

You cannot lose yourself by remembering
your divine connection with all living things.

An occasional show of kindness does not make someone kind.
Love is dependable. Be someone you can count on.

Acts of love, hope and mindfulness shed light on the past,
transform the present and invite brighter tomorrows.

The dawn breaks even the darkest of nights. Awaken from darkness, watch a baby day being born and know there is always hope, always love, always a road to peace.

One small step after another can take you just about anywhere.

Life is an endless story, full of beginnings, adventures and completions. Embrace it, love it, be it, invent it, create it, believe it, dramatise it, write about it, meditate on it, breathe it, be healed and invigorated by it, be joyful because of it … and above all remember that you are it.

You are the rise and the fall, the ebb and the flow, never to be repeated, ungraspable, infinite, eternal and omnipresent.

*Listen to and respect all points of view. But in the end,
be responsible to your own truths.*

*In the arms of Mother Earth, you can find acceptance, clarity,
strength and beauty you can depend on.*

*The mountain tops, the valleys and the stars follow the same
natural laws as grains of sand. It is nature's loyalty to these laws
that gives Earth the order it needs to support life.*

Before you accept a truth as absolute, put it to the test. Is it as true for the weak as it is for the strong? Is it as right for the rich as it is for the poor? The laws of the universe have no bias. We can depend of them regardless of age, wealth, culture or status.

Give yourself the opportunity to absorb higher thinking,
greater visions and deeper love.

Increase your focus on love, and it will naturally flow out into the world, following the channels of concentration to where it is needed most. The energy you foster in yourself and in the world is a choice. Be selective. Choose love.

EARTH SONG

of time and space
and all that is spaceless

of trees glowing
in my heart
and wildflowers

spreading through vast green
yellow fields
and spaces

of seasons past
and those yet to come

of oceans
unfolding
memories

and the gentle breeze

that blows
softly
caressingly

surrounding
embracing
recollecting

gathering
fading
into yesterday's light

of this all absorbing life
and dream

and death
and of coming
and going

and of all things eternal
like the soul

of atoms of energy
flowing through the vast
spaceless space of infinity

and the earth beneath my feet
the stars in your eyes
and moss
and leaves of the forest

and love …

— Toni Carmine Salerno

Imagination can be your greatest asset if you value and nurture it. This requires some daydreaming, playfulness and light-heartedness. Let your imagination guide you to new ways of seeing and being in the world. The resources you need are all around you, so take the mundane and transform your world into something magical.

Poke, dare and test your expectations. If something is real,
it will remain. Truth doesn't mind being questioned.
Sometimes we need to let go of what we know to make way for wisdom.

The process of self-discovery deepens and strengthens your spiritual connection to life, Earth and the universe. Gradually, you will come to your own truths, and gradually you will let them go, as you embrace deeper, more profound realisations. Every precious, miraculous moment of your life has the capacity to transform you.

Once upon a time, around four billion years ago, a solar nebula collapsed and spun in on itself. Our Sun formed at its centre, and what remained of the nebula orbited around it. The push and pull of gravity worked its magic, merging heavier objects with smaller ones, until our solar system was formed. In the beginning, powerful transformation can look like chaos. If an aspect of your world seems to implode and crash in on itself, or if you feel things are spinning out of control, remember this is a process, not the destination. Once the dust settles, whole new worlds and systems will be available to you.

When all around you changes, as it most surely will, love will remain.

The mountain watches the comings and goings of time. Snow or fire may ravage its surface, but its centre is unchanged. Ice drifts into streams that reach to the oceans. Ash sinks into soil and rekindles growth. You are a mountain. The comings and goings of life might rage on the surface, but your centre is strong, watchful and enduring. Harsh words, criticisms and doubts are like pebbles. They might be flung your way, and you may notice them, but they cannot touch your core. The mountain is anchored deep in the earth and rises beyond the clouds. Feel the sure footings of your foundation. Connect to your centre, which cannot be rocked. Rise to your lofty heights and look out on forever.

There are parts of yourself you are yet to realise.
Take your time getting to know them.

You have nothing to prove, nothing to hide.
You are blessed and held in the loving field of the Divine Mother.

Let the truth reveal itself.

Don't confuse stability with stagnation. Movement is constant.
Be sure to direct it.

Beyond the theories, assumptions and limitations of the manifested world lies a truer reality. Still your mind, focus on your heart centre and allow the wisdom of the ages to illuminate your thoughts, nurture your soul and guide you to wholeness.

Believing the earth is flat doesn't make it so, but it does create false limitations and impede your journey. Likewise, believing you are unworthy, unlovable or incapable doesn't make it so, but it will create false limits. Be conscious of the thoughts, opinions and values that are steering your journey.

You can talk yourself in circles but remain unheard. At other times, you can be heard without uttering a word. The onus of understanding is on the listener. Love, care and consideration are expressed by an attentive ear and a welcoming heart.

Tone, pitch, tremolo and words are just sound in empty space
until the moment they are heard.

Generate a positively charged self-image through conscious, affirmative action.

The consequences of your actions extend beyond your immediate sphere.
The stronger the action, the greater the influence.

Look within, and you will see that love is not a distant shore,
but an ocean of light inside you.

Putting your toe in the water won't tell you how salty it is.

Shifting a single limiting belief will release a flood of creativity, insight and confidence. Replace hoping for change with acting for change.

Setting a goal or a dream in motion is not a mysterious undertaking, it is mechanical — it requires action. The act of study moves ignorance to knowledge. A first attempt brings you closer to achievement.

Your underlying motives — the forces that compel you — may determine your direction, but it is your actions that take you there.

Stop and learn a lesson so you can move forward.

Nature's patterns are responsive, intelligent and reliable, but not predictable. You are a unique expression of spiralling DNA, but you are not limited by your patterning. You have all the time you need to understand the patterns in your world. You also have the power to change them.

What else might we sense about the world if we could
hone our ability to perceive it?

You are you in your own free and glorious expression, not a reflection of circumstance, expectation or assumption. Define and trust yourself.

From the calm, neutral perspective of love, free from the fear, guilt and judgement of this world, your higher self looks through the conflict and drama of the physical world and sees meaning and purpose.

From a distance, chaos looks perfectly ordered.

The one thing
we all have in common
is that we are all different
but only slightly different
for we are all part of the same tapestry
this is why there are over seven billion truths in the world today
and every day new truths are born
because everyone of us is part of the truth
each holds their own piece of the truth
no one person holds all the truth
that is why we can never agree on anything
until we join together and agree that it's all right to disagree.

— Toni Carmine Salerno

A glass of water is colourless, but an ocean of water is blue.
Air is colourless, but a sky full of air is blue. Little things you
brush off as nothing compound and colour your world.

Use whatever life sends you to your advantage. You can sit on the potential within you, or you can release it. It is not a matter of circumstance, ability or worthiness. It is your choice. Convert a possibility into reality.

As we release our hidden potentials, we create our destiny.

Energy is neither negative nor positive but can be used in any number of ways. Electricity can be used to hurt or return someone to life. There is potential in everything ... in your memories, your hopes, your doubts, your fears, your strengths. How you use that potential is up to you.

It is okay to take your time.

With a little work and perspective, an obstacle can become a stepping stone.

Convert the lessons and experiences you have absorbed into life-giving creativity. There is joy in productivity. Its nectar is sweetly intoxicating and its fruit is a mark of transformation and completeness.

The capacity to interpret our reactions with awareness is distinctly human. Not responding to your world is not possible. Expecting to manage, control, deny or drive your feelings out of existence is like continuously turning up the heat and being surprised when the water boils. Uncomfortable emotions are powerful signals. Listen to them.

Confidence is certain to give success its best shot.

A mountain ash can become five thousand times bigger than the seed it began as.
But this is not the seed's concern. Its job is to give the plant embryo its best start.

Your body remembers. Listen to its story. Be gentle with who you were and strong about who you will become.

Giving something a try is not a lifelong obligation. You can switch, swap and refine your interests, friends, lovers, career, plans and home as often as you like. If something doesn't fit right, try something new — and if that doesn't work out, try something else. There is no failure in moving on or starting over.

Your heart holds your truth in every breath. What does it say?
Listen and you shall be reborn.

Footprints in the snow, shapes in the clouds, tracks in the ice all disappear
like they never were. Life makes its mark with no obligation,
no expectation. A masterpiece is lost beneath the next snowfall.
Refreshing, perpetual renewal is here, now, always, awaiting you.

Your thoughts and actions draw from the past and feed your future.
The journey repeats as often as needed. There is no rushing through to the
end. The cycle can be broken through wisdom, detachment, a memory of
the sacred or a return to oneness.

The memory of creation is stored within the ground you walk on. Still your mind, relax, close your eyes and feel the timeless healing energy of our Mother Earth.

Mother Nature faces environmental pressure with ingenuity,
and you are empowered to do the same.

Adversity quickens growth and adaptation and is followed by confidence, strength and stability. Acknowledge your capacity to flourish through challenge.

It is neither too soon nor too late to claim your life for yourself.

There is no shame in changing your mind or walking away from a person or belief. Some things are meant for a lifetime, but others can only offer temporary solace or fleeting fulfilment. Do not cling to the moment, nor to the stepping stone.

Space exists within and without an object. Space is both a container and a boundary. Without space, there would be no separation ... the entire universe would be one solid mass. There would be no growth, no change, no evolution. Space gives us room to know who we are within, but separate to, the world around us. Yes, we are all from the same infinite source, part of a complete and magical universe, but we are also uniquely complete and magical beings. Space empowers us with boundaries, individuality and freedom. Respecting these gifts honours all of creation.

Give up the idea that you must be good at everything. Narrowing your interests and building on your strengths will conserve output and increase your value.

Step outside of competition and create new ways for yourself and others to flourish.

Holding yourself back is counterintuitive. Doubt, fear, anxiety and grief may be part of your journey, but they are not the journey. Stretch, grow and LIVE!

In a fleeting moment of grace, in the space between your thoughts, you may glimpse a silent bliss that is beyond words or description. This all-encompassing love is your soulful, spiritual centre. It is without beginning or end. Reach for it, and this state of grace shall be a guiding light in this world and beyond. It is life. It is eternal.

All that you reach for is transformed into growth.

Position yourself towards all that is life-affirming — words, foods, activities, hobbies, songs, images. Grasp for goodness, grow beyond the shade and be fruitful. A seedling doesn't grow beyond the canopy overnight. It gets there by consistently seeking the light that is just out of reach.

We are all a little messy beneath the surface.
(And that's where the gold, gemstones and other treasures are!)

Earth doesn't know what day or millennium it is. The calendar we follow means nothing to her. It is a construct — a filter through which we perceive our age or measure our progress through life. The sunrise doesn't wait for an alarm to ring. Life isn't measured by ticks and tocks. How old would you be if you didn't know your age? If there was no such thing as 'too early', 'too late' or 'one day', would it change how you see yourself?

*Peace is not somewhere in the future, it is here. You don't need to
search for it. Trust, let go, be present ... and it will find you.*

*All existing matter and energy appeared and exploded from a single
point. Simple elements pulled together to form giant stars. These
exploded to birth galaxies. In one of those galaxies, a cloud of dust
and debris fell into orbit around a dwarf star. That dust formed
the planets of our solar system. On one of those planets, life began.
Consciousness arose. You came to be here. Amazing!*